Seeing Both Sides

Learning a Second Language, Yes or No

Kevin Walker

Rourke
Educational Media
rourkeeducationalmedia.com

Scan for Related Titles
and Teacher Resources

Before Reading:

Building Academic Vocabulary and Background Knowledge

Before reading a book, it is important to tap into what your child or students already know about the topic. This will help them develop their vocabulary, increase their reading comprehension, and make connections across the curriculum.

1. Look at the cover of the book. What will this book be about?
2. What do you already know about the topic?
3. Let's study the Table of Contents. What will you learn about in the book's chapters?
4. What would you like to learn about this topic? Do you think you might learn about it from this book? Why or why not?
5. Use a reading journal to write about your knowledge of this topic. Record what you already know about the topic and what you hope to learn about the topic.
6. Read the book.
7. In your reading journal, record what you learned about the topic and your response to the book.
8. After reading the book complete the activities below.

Content Area Vocabulary
Read the list. What do these words mean?

circumstances
complex
diplomat
eliminate
fluent
foreign
interactive
interpret
sequence
translate

After Reading:

Comprehension and Extension Activity

After reading the book, work on the following questions with your child or students in order to check their level of reading comprehension and content mastery.

1. What is an opinion? (Summarize)
2. How do personal experiences shape someone's opinion? (Infer)
3. Why would anyone oppose learning something new? (Asking questions)
4. How might learning a second language affect your daily life? (Text to self connection)
5. Is school the only place someone can learn a second language? (Asking questions)

Extension Activity

Once you've written about your opinion on learning a second language, create a brochure that highlights your best points. Think about other brochures you've seen that are designed to sell something. You want to sell your opinion! You can add research statistics, quotes from classmates, pictures, and anything else that supports your side.

Table of Contents

Taking Sides

Every year, students across the United States take **foreign** language classes. People have different opinions about whether learning a second language is valuable. They form their opinions by thinking about their own beliefs and experiences. They also consider facts and information about the topic.

Reality ✓

The top foreign languages studied in U.S. high schools are Spanish, French, and German.

Do you have an opinion about learning a second language? Is it an important skill for students to learn or is their time better spent learning something else?

Explaining your opinion about a **complex** topic requires research, facts, and information. Here are two opinions on language studies. Check out what each has to say. Then it's your turn to decide!

Learning a Second Language? Yes, Please!

Learning a second language is important for students. The world is more connected than ever before and knowing a language other than your own creates many opportunities.

Speaking a foreign language is also fun. Imagine going to another country and understanding signs, menus, and communicating with people in their native language.

Reality ✓

Mexico, Canada, the United Kingdom, France, Italy, and Germany are the countries most visited by people from the U.S.

Young people who learn a second language perform better on important tests, especially in math, reading, and vocabulary. This includes tests students take to get into college.

Learning a second language also can help you remember a **sequence** or list of items. Some researchers have found that it even makes your brain grow!

One study looked at brain patterns before and after learning a foreign language. It found that important parts of the brain actually increased in volume. This was especially true in parts of the brain that help you form language skills.

Foreign language learners are better listeners. Studies have found that they have a better partnership between hearing and brain functions. In other words, learning a new language makes you better at hearing what others are saying.

Scientists have found that people who are able to speak a second language are better at switching from one task to another. This is because their brain shows more flexibility and can better handle sudden, unexpected **circumstances**.

While learning a second language, you open yourself up to talking to people you might otherwise never meet. Being able to speak to someone in their native language means you can get to know them better.

If you learn Spanish, French, or German, you can travel to many parts of the world and not need someone to **translate** for you.

Knowing how to speak to someone in their own language also helps you learn about different places, cultures, and customs. That means you will have a better understanding of the world. How can that be a bad thing?

After students graduate, they need to find jobs. As the world becomes more **interactive**, it becomes more important for workers to speak a second language. It is an asset many companies look for when hiring people.

Reality ✓

An estimated 4.5 to 6.5 million United States citizens work in other countries.

Almost every profession will require you to interact with people who live in other parts of the world. Knowing a second language will make you more open to other cultures and ways of life.

Anyone can learn a second language. Some students take to it faster than others and things click for them quickly. However, even those who have problems at first can succeed with practice and perseverance.

Reality ✓

About 80 percent of public schools have had funding cuts since 2008, according to U.S. News and World Report. Some of the first programs to get cut are music, art, and foreign language.

Funding for learning a second language is sometimes cut when schools run low on money. With all the benefits that foreign language studies give students, those cuts could be damaging to your future in the workplace.

Much like music programs, learning a second language opens up a whole new way of looking at the world. Speaking a second language can be as important to students as learning math or history.

There are too many positive effects from learning a second language to ignore. And based on scientific research and the experiences of those who know a second language, it's easy to see how important it is to learn one!

ONUM
MANE

Bonjour

HELLO
guten
morgen

Labas
rytas

buenos
días
sabah

BOM DIA

Dobrý
den

Buongiorno

Learning a Second Language? No Way!

Learning a second language might help you have more fun on your vacation, but for those who don't plan to travel to other countries, knowing only your native language is enough.

English-speaking tourists have always traveled to places where another language is spoken. They can get along fine with a translation book or by hiring someone to **interpret** for them.

Why should students waste time and schools waste money teaching students something that is really not all that useful? Shouldn't they focus more on learning about science, technology, engineering, and math?

Surely those subjects are more important than knowing how to properly ask someone for directions to a restaurant or attraction in another language.

Reality ✓

There is a shortage of workers in the United States in science, technology, engineering, and math. Job vacancies for workers in these fields stay open twice as long as other jobs.

Only about 30 percent of Americans have passports, and more than half have never traveled outside the country, so learning another language isn't necessary for the majority of U.S. citizens.

Many people point to the global economy as a reason for learning a second language. They say many jobs will require working with people in other countries. However, most U.S. students will work in the United States, where English is the most-spoken language.

If you think you want to become a foreign **diplomat** or work in the foreign office of a large corporation, then maybe it is worthwhile. But knowing a second language doesn't necessarily mean you'll make more money. One study found that it just adds about two percent to what you get paid every year.

Research has shown that only about one in every 100 students who take foreign language classes in school becomes **fluent** in the language. You must have someone to speak with on a constant basis to retain what you have learned.

Many people in the world learn English because so much business is conducted by English-speaking countries. Learning English can lead to better jobs. The reverse may not be true for most people in the United States.

The number of people learning English around the world will reach two billion by 2020, according to researchers.

Reality ✓

About 3.2 billion people around the world will use the Internet this year, according to the United Nations. That's almost half the total world population of 7.2 billion.

Part of the reason for more people learning English is the Internet. English is the most common language on almost 55 percent of the top websites worldwide. The second is Russian, which is used on about six percent of the websites.

After the Great Recession began in 2008, many schools had to cut foreign language programs. That's because they depend on funding from the government to pay for their operations, and the government has less money when fewer people are paying taxes.

Reality ✓

At least 35 of the 50 states still provide less funding for schools than they did before 2008.

With such tight budgets, the money schools do have would be better spent giving raises to teachers or focusing on more worthwhile studies.

For example, the public school district in Chicago, Illinois, had to **eliminate** 1,400 jobs in 2015 and cut $200 million from the budget. That's a lot of jobs and a lot of money.

Some school districts have eliminated most or all field trips. Isn't seeing a museum or historical site in person more important than speaking a second language?

Teaching foreign languages is expensive for schools and takes time away from other, more important subjects. Learning a second language does little to help your economic future.

Students are better off studying subjects that can increase their opportunities for successful careers.

Your Turn

Now that you have read arguments for and against learning a second language, what is your opinion? Both sides used facts, research, and experience to present their thoughts. Which one do you think did a better job? Are there things either side could have said but didn't?

Now comes the fun part – sharing your thoughts about the topic. Write about your opinion using facts, details, and examples from your own experiences.

Telling Your Side: Writing Opinion Pieces

- Tell your opinion first. Use phrases such as:
- *I like _____.*
- *I think_____.*
- *_____ is the best _____.*
- Give multiple reasons to support your opinion. Use facts and relevant information instead of stating your feelings.
- Use the words *and, because,* and *also* to connect your opinion to your reasons.
- Clarify or explain your facts by using the phrases *for example* or *such as.*
- Compare your opinion to a different opinion. Then point out reasons that your opinion is better. You can use phrases such as:
- *Some people think_____, but I disagree because _____.*
- *_____ is better than _____ because _____.*
- Give examples of positive outcomes if the reader agrees with your opinion. For example, you can use the phrase, *If _____ then _____.*
- Use a personal story about your own experiences with your topic. For example, if you are writing about your opinion on after-school sports, you can write about your own experiences after-school sports activities.
- Finish your opinion piece with a strong conclusion that highlights your strongest arguments. Restate your opinion so your reader remembers how you feel.

Glossary

circumstances (SUR-kuhm-stan-sez): the facts or conditions that are connected to an event

complex (KAHM-plex): very complicated

diplomat (DIP-luh-mat): someone who officially represents his or her country's government in a foreign country as a job

eliminate (i-LIM-uh-nate): to leave out or get rid of

fluent (FLOO-uhnt): able to speak easily and well

foreign (FOR-uhn): of, having to do with, or coming from another country

interactive (in-tur-AK-tiv): working together or influencing each other

interpret (in-TUR-prit): to translate a conversation from one language to another

sequence (SEE-kwuhns): following of one thing after another in a regular or fixed order

translate (trans-LATE): to change spoken or written words from one language to another

Index

Show What You Know

1. What languages are studied the most by students in the United States?

2. What countries do people from the United States travel to the most?

3. How does learning a foreign language improve your brain?

4. How many people in the United States have passports?

5. What is the most common language on the world's most popular Internet sites?

Websites to Visit

www.chillola.com

www.learnalanguage.com

www.timeforkids.com/homework-helper/a-plus-papers/
   persuasive-essay

About the Author

Kevin Walker is a writer, editor, and father. He likes to hear kids' opinions because they are always honest and also often very funny. He lives in Houston, Texas, where you can get some of best tacos in the world. That's a good thing.

Meet The Author!
www.meetREMauthors.com

PHOTO CREDITS: Cover (top): ©Aldo Murillo; cover (bottom): ©Patrick Foto; page 1, 8, 14, 28: ©Global Stock; page 3: ©Christopher Futcher; page 4, 9, 18, 23, 25, 27: ©Susan Chiang; page 4, 6, 13, 14, 18, 23, 24: ©loops7; page 5: ©Dougberry; page 6: ©andresr; page 7: ©monkeybusinessimages; page 10: ©rez-art; page 11: ©Cathy Yeulet; page 12: ©BraunS; page 13: ©LiudmylasSupynska; page 15: ©Kate_Sept2004; page 16: ©Gpointstudio; page 17: ©Andrejs Zemdega; page 19: ©Sturti; page 20: ©michaeljung; page 21: ©Steve Debenport; page 22: ©Oktay Ortakciogiu; page 24: ©Mangesn Ambetak; page 26: ©Ulrikje Hammerich; page 29: ©Sezeryadigar

Edited by: Keli Sipperley

Cover design by: Rhea Magaro
Interior design by: Tara Raymo

Library of Congress PCN Data

Learning a Second Language, Yes or No / Kevin Walker
(Seeing Both Sides)
ISBN 978-1-68191-386-5 (hard cover)
ISBN 978-1-68191-428-2 (soft cover)
ISBN 978-1-68191-468-8 (e-Book)
Library of Congress Control Number: 2015951554

Also Available as:

ROURKE'S
e-Books

Printed in the United States of America, North Mankato, Minnesota